Gary Legwold

The Last Toast to
Lutefisk!

The Last Toast to
Lutefisk!

102 TOASTS, TIDBITS, AND TRIFLES
FOR YOUR NEXT LUTEFISK DINNER

By GARY LEGWOLD

Illustrations by PETER KRAUSE

Conrad Henry Press
Minneapolis, 1999

The Last Toast to Lutefisk!
102 Toasts, Tidbits, and Trifles
for Your Next Lutefisk Dinner

Text copyright 1999 Gary Legwold

Illustration copyright 1999 Gary Legwold and Peter Krause

Published by:

Conrad Henry Press

5205 Knox Avenue South

Minneapolis, MN 55419-1041

1-888-LUTEFIS or 1-888-588-3347 (toll free)

Web site: http://www.lutefisk.com

E-mail: glegwold@lutefisk.com

ISBN 0-9652027-1-2

Library of Congress Catalog Card Number: 99-65890

To Hank, who called me "Hot Shot."
Your humor will be missed.

Acknowledgments

I am grateful to humor itself for lightening the load and making this book so enjoyable to write.

Thanks Earl Hipp, Dave Hintzman, and Cris Anderson. You unknowingly contributed your quirky sense of humor to this quirky little book.

Thanks to Donna Burch at Stanton Publication Services for her design work and nice touches.

Thanks also to Peter Krause, whose warm and spirited illustrations on the covers and inside the book bring to life the book's humor. We met on the first tee of the Hiawatha Golf Course in Minneapolis. Finding him on that windy, April day was better than a hole-in-one (although I wish I'd get an ace, just so I could do an honest comparison).

Finally, thanks to Kathy Weflen, who edited the book, as she did *The Last Word on Lutefisk*. As editor, she serves as Taste Control. Sometimes, my humor strays over the line, into the Tasteless Zone.

Quietly, but firmly, she reels me back—or at least requires that I warn the reader. In short, she has good sense. So, here's a toast to you, Kathy:

To lutefisk: It makes a lot of scents.

Contents

The Last Toast to
Lutefisk!

A Toast to Randi

A toast is one of those universal gestures that has the power to lift, to raise what appears to be a simple moment with friends and loved ones to a memorable time. A sincere, well-offered toast is an appeal to all gathered to pause and appreciate. The presenter asks us to listen and reflect on this poem, prayer, proverb, roast, boast, or show of wit. It is a scene you cherish long after the evening is spent.

I must admit that, until recently, I had never given the art of toasting much thought. The toasts I had heard at weddings and anniversaries were usually bumbled or boring or bawdy (in striking contrast to the few I have presented, which were brilliant and becoming). Toasts, with rare exceptions, were to be tolerated; they were speed bumps on the road to good food. That was my thinking until I went to a friend's house for lutefisk dinner one wintry night.

As night fell, winter grinned, confident that its weight would crush all civility, mingling, and merriment. No one would venture out on this January eve. Winter, winking at death itself, had won. Its numbing cold and haughty wind made us Minnesotans wary and weary, resigned to isolate and insulate ourselves against such arctic conditions.

Just as I was starting to feel good and sorry for myself, I remembered I had booked a lutefisk dinner for that night. I groaned. Jane, my wife, groaned. The windows rattled and frost furred up on the panes. So tempting it was to hunker down and only come up for spring.

But this was not any old lutefisk dinner. This was the annual feast of Odd Unstad. From his native Lofoten Islands in Norway, Odd imports dried cod sticks—the real stuff, not ling cod like you eat at church or lodge dinners. In his basement he soaks the cod in water, then in water laced with lye, then in water again. After about three weeks of soaking, the fish is ready to be cooked; then Odd invites his dearest friends to dinner at his lakeside home in Shorewood, Minn. The invited guests, many of them fellow Norwegian immigrants, know lutefisk, its history, its tradition, its lore. To sit at Odd's table is a rite of winter, a ceremony that allows us to thumb our nose at the worst of the season. On this night, Jane and I decided to buck up and be brave. We were going for lutefisk.

We arrived and entered Odd's home, stomping snow off our boots. Odd, wearing a red lutefisk chef's hat autographed by his friends, greeted us and took our coats. We joined the dozen others for cocktails, including my annual martini with three olives.

It was so good to see Randi, Odd's wife. She gave

Jane a hug. These two had become friends with an unusual but special bond. Randi, who graced the cover of my second book, *The Last Word on Lutefisk,* was receiving treatments for breast cancer. Jane's mother and two sisters have had breast cancer and mastectomies. Two years before this dinner, Jane chose to have prophylactic mastectomies. After years of research and consulting with doctors, Jane was sure, given her family history, that she would develop breast cancer. So she elected to have both breasts removed and thereby reduce the risk—and her fear—immensely. Randi applauded Jane's decision each time they talked at these dinners.

That night would be the last we would see Randi alive. In a year she would succumb to the cancer. And at our next lutefisk dinner at Odd's, I would rise and offer a toast to Randi's memory.

But I get ahead of myself. At this dinner, we relished the present, feeling the warmth, filling our glasses, and oozing our best charm. Lutefisk exercised its power to alert our wind-chilled senses, yank us back to now, and help us lighten up. We shared laughter and spirit and anticipation of this singular fish and all the trimmings.

Randi seated us at the candlelit table and offered aquavit and Heineken beer. Behind the sliding door, in the kitchen, Odd piled lutefisk filets on the serving dish. Ceremoniously, he opened the door and emerged to "aahs" and "oohs." The fish had arrived—steaming. We passed the lutefisk, as well as potatoes sprinkled with parsley, rutabagas, butter, flatbread, and melted butter laced with sautéed onions and bacon.

Amid laughter and chatter and cross talk and sips of aquavit, we filled our plates. And just when it appeared that we were ready to indulge in this fantastic meal, we paused, expectantly. The toast. Surely, someone would offer a toast. We waited silently. Finally, Odd rose.

He raised a glass to his friends, as he had done many times before. But this year, we all realized the poignancy of his simple toast. We did not know how long Randi would live. Who can know such a thing, cancer or no? But we did know a simple truth: As our loved ones pass on, our friends keep us going. Of course, he did not say all this. He didn't have to. He gave a toast that honored the possibilities of life, including the opportunity for friends to gather at the table to eat this fabled fish. He raised his glass and we raised ours, in unison, as if picking the fruit that held this sweet moment.

Randi Unstad

Photo: Doug Baartman

A Bit of Toasting Know-How

Driving home from the Unstad lutefisk dinner, I began to think about toasts. How heartfelt the toasts had been, I said to Jane. How simple and yet how moving they can be. And how sad that the tradition of toasting seems to be slipping away.

Perhaps the desire to honor friends and tradition is why I decided to devote a book to toasting. My first books, *The Last Word on Lefse* and *The Last Word on Lutefisk,* were about traditional Scandinavian foods that are in danger of dying out. My goal was, and is, to help preserve them by writing about the people who still cherish the heritage and are energized by these heritage foods. I want my books to be used, if you will, as a breakwater to protect our eroding cultural shoreline.

Toasting, of course, extends far beyond the Scandinavian heritage. And casting a lifeline to this sinking tradition is for more than heritage reasons. I just like toasts, I guess. I am a writer, and I like the toast's playful and inventive use of language. I like what toasting does for the people who receive them and for those who give them. A toast can make us blush and reflect and laugh and cry. A toast can be sentimental, cynical, lyric, comic, and defiant. A toast forces us to search our heart and express its contents. Toasts beg us to look for the best, for the most endearing and most enduring considerations. "They are the medium through which such deep feelings as love, hope, high spirits, and admiration can be quickly, conveniently, and sincerely expressed," writes Paul Dickson in his book *Toasts: Over 1,500 of the Best Toasts, Sentiments, Blessings, and Graces.*

According to Dickson, the decline of this rich form of expression began about a third of the way into this century and continues to this day. It is hard to say why. Perhaps people entertain less and eat fast food more. Perhaps people have reduced the meal to feeding—forget the festivities. Perhaps people are reading less and therefore lack the facility with words that is required for an eloquent toast. Whatever the causes, Dickson says 20th century people have "less time and inclination to work them up or memorize them."

However, "there was a time, not that long ago," he writes, "when one could not go to a luncheon—let alone a banquet or wedding—without hearing a series of carefully proposed and executed toasts. Toasts were the test of one's ability to come up with an appropriate inspiration to sip to the honor of some person, sentiment, or institution. It really didn't matter if it was an original written for the occasion or a time-tested classic passed down from Elizabethan times. What was important was whether or not the toast worked to keep the proceedings moving at a jolly pace."

At a lutefisk dinner such as those hosted by the Unstads, there is little risk of proceedings not moving at a jolly pace. But if there were, invariably someone in the middle of the meal would clink a glass and raise a toast. These toasts typically begin as expressions of gratitude to Randi and Odd for their hospitality. Sincere stuff that is followed by some sort of segue (not necessarily smooth) to a joke.

Sometimes the joke is on the raunchy side. For example, at one dinner Patrick Corbett told this "Ole and Lena" joke: Ole is noticing that Lena has put on weight, maybe from eating too much lutefisk. One day Ole is crabby and tells Lena that her back side is getting as broad as a Weber kettle grill. Lena lets it pass—for now. Come Saturday night, Ole is in an amorous mood and suggests to Lena that they go to the bedroom to make beautiful music together. Lena, she thinks about this, then says with a smile, "Why, Ole, you don't think I would heat up my big Weber grill for one little weenie, do you?"

The joke illustrates that toasters tend to wander away from the high road. And that is usually OK, if done in moderation and with some sense of taste. Indeed, the potential for danger and innuendo is part of the appeal of a toast. But always keep in mind that toasting is not the same as being a stand-up comic. A toast may include a joke, but a toast is not just a joke.

Before proceeding on to the 102 toasts, tidbits, and trifles, let's do a bit about how to toast. Toasting has a long history (some of which you will learn of in this book) and a short set of guidelines. These guidelines, listed below, will help you present an effective toast. They need not be strictly followed and are often overridden by or adapted to local custom.

For example, Scandinavians have a very personal, intimate toasting ritual, which you might follow or adapt. Before saying the toast, the toaster, sitting or standing, raises a full glass in the right hand to the point at the chest where the third button down on a military tunic would be located. "The toaster's eyes seek out a companionate partner, using the raised glass and brooding gaze as a veritable beacon," writes Robert L. Garrison in his book *Here's to You: 354 Toasts You Can Use Today for Parties, Holidays, and Public Affairs.*

Once eye contact is established, the toasters share a smile, nod their heads, and say "Skoal!" They drain their glasses if they are drinking aquavit, or sip if the drink is wine. They lower their glasses to the original position, lock eyes again, nod, and the toast is complete.

This intimate toast can be used at a dinner party. The host first gives a "Skoal" to all the guests, who are expected to return the courtesy to the host and then the other guests. The hostess is not expected to be the "most" with the toasts. She may make token responses to several toasts at a time, "thus cutting down on her alcoholic intake and lessening the risk of burned biscuits," writes Garrison.

Speaking of aquavit, Garrison writes of a Danish drink that skoalers use. It is called "a little black one," made by placing a small silver coin in the bottom of an empty coffee cup. You add black coffee until the coin disappears. Then you add akvavit (Danish spelling) until the coffee thins enough so that the coin reappears. Then you offer a toast, usually at the end of the feast.

Whether you toast Scandinavian style or create your own rituals for your lutefisk dinners, do it with style. That is perhaps the best point to remember. Remember also, as a point of order, that the etiquette is to permit the host to open the toasting. Then chime in. Lutefisk dinners are not burdened with such toasting protocal as you will find at weddings and affairs of state. At weddings, for example, the first toast is made by the best man. The groom customarily responds by thanking the best man, parents, and in-laws. The bride may then wish to make her own toast. This is followed by the couple's parents, members of the wedding party, family members, and guests.

However, this is not a wedding toast book. The toasting you will do at lutefisk dinners is quite informal. If you have a toast in your heart, wait for the host's toast and then say your own. That's the bottom line. To help you say it with as much style as possible, here are a few other toasting tips:

- **Be prepared**. Work carefully on the creation or selection of a toast. Start preparing a week or two before the dinner. Stand in front of a mirror and deliver your toast. Have it memorized and polished by the time dinner is served. You want your audience to be fully attentive to your sentiments, not focused on the note cards in your shaking hands.

- **Be original**. Look at the toast as special, distinctive, and memorable. Toasts can be an original composition or gleaned from other people's anecdotes, jokes, stories, verse, and quotations. Michel de Montaigne once said, "I quote others only the better to express myself." Expression is the whole point in a toast. In spite of the value of well-chosen quotations, I encourage you to try expressing yourself in your own words, using your own ideas. Many toasters find that their enthusiasm for toasting flings open the curtain of modesty, revealing the writer, speaker, dramatist, and humorist within.

- **Be yourself**. The best toasts are simple and from your heart. Be witty, be eloquent, be dignified, be commanding, be creative, be funny, but do it in character true to yourself.

- **Be brief**. Sages such as Shakespeare have said, "Brevity is the soul of wit." As you prepare, time your toast. While there is no time limit, as a general guideline remember the words of George Jessel, "If you haven't struck oil in your first three minutes, stop boring!"

- **Be upbeat**. Rise and give the toast. You may be nervous about making your presentation, but act as upbeat as possible. You can do this! You are prepared, and your audience is very forgiving. They want you to do well.

Just as there are dos, so there are don'ts:

1) Don't raise your glass when you are the one being toasted. That would be like applauding for yourself. If you want to raise a glass, do it and say thanks when the toast is completed and the fanfare dies down.
2) Don't toast the guest of honor before the host has the chance.
3) Finally, don't stare at the lutefisk.

In the interest of full disclosure, I should say something about the origins of the toasts that follow. Most of them are original, or at least they came out of my head. However, I humbly keep in mind the words of Franklin P. Jones: "Originality is the art of concealing your source." For some of these toasts, the source is the wisdom of the men and women who have recorded their toasts in books. I admit I have slanted a few here and there to the lutefisk dinner crowd. So there you have it.

But just as I am about to feel bad about this borrowing, the *Bible* bails me out. For, as it says in Ecclesiastes, there is nothing new under the sun. And wasn't it Auguste Rodin who said, "I invent nothing. I rediscover."? Well, I have rediscovered some great old toasts and tried my best to change their wording so they could fly at your next lutefisk dinner.

On with the toasts, including this one:

Here's to lutefisk, to lefse, to friends, and to love.
May you have plenty on this earth
and more up above!

Toasts, Tidbits, and Trifles

To the taste of lutefisk:

Do not resist it—many are denied the privilege.

~

To friends, as long as we are able,
We'll serve lutefisk from this table.

~

To apprehension and lutefisk:

Be happy my friend, hang easy and loose
Getting tense 'bout lutefisk is just no use.
It goes down, tastes good, and makes you feel well,
Providing (ahem) that you get past the smell.

~

To impatience:

Good fish, a good seat
Good God, sit and eat!

~

Up to my lips and down to my soul
Lutefisk—fill me, this is my goal.

~

To proper planning:

May this lovely repast
Keep us alive
Ten of us for dinner,
Lutefisk for five.

~

A bit of history:

The ancient Greeks drank to one's health as an assurance to visiting dignitaries that the drink was not spiked with poison. The host drank from the cup first to prove the offered drink was not harmful, which generated feelings of trust and good will.

May our table always be too small
to seat all our friends.

~

To folks who kinda like lutefisk:

Our house is kinda simple
Our table kinda plain.
This fish is kinda kooky
Our guests are kinda sane.

~

To God who gives us fish
To lutefisk, a tasty dish
To a careful chef, we have one wish
Don't overcook, or this is ISH!

~

A bit of history:

When Cleopatra was entertaining Marc Anthony on her
Nile River barge, she dropped two perfect pearls into her
wine. She then offered a toast to his health, and drank
down the wine and pearls.

A tasteless joke for lutefisk eaters who like football:

Two Green Bay Packers fans were seated next to a Minnesota Vikings fan at a lutefisk dinner. The Vikings fan must have had a problem because he kept excusing himself to go to the bathroom.

The Packers fans, being the prankish sort, spit on the Vikings fan's lutefisk when he went to the bathroom. He returned, took a bite of lutefisk, and did not seem to notice the spit.

The next time the Vikings fan left the table, the Packers fans asked him to please return with two beers. Again, the Packers fans spit on the Vikings fan's lutefisk.

The Vikings fan returned with two foamy glasses of beer, which the Packers fans drank with great satisfaction. The Vikings fan sat down and took another bite of lutefisk. With a look of disgust, he said, "How long must this go on? Why can't we rivals live in peace? What causes Packers and Vikings fans to stoop to such lowliness that we spit on each other's lutefisk and pee in each other's beers?"

To the church worker or anyone brave enough to try lutefisk for the first time:

Here's to the soul whose intentions are clear
To risk heartburn and doom without showing fear.
Let's rise everyone and let us all cheer
To the toast that I give this brave volunteer.

～

To bad lutefisk, bad wine, or bad poetry:

'Tis hard to tell which is worse
The food, the drink, or another verse.

～

To lutefisk:

An undertaker disguised as fish.

～

To lutefisk eaters of any old age:

Wisdom is curious and asks, "But why?"
When you eat this fish.
Wisdom inquires, "Do you want to die—
Is this your one last wish?"

~

May you eat lutefisk for 100 years
and I be at the table to count them.

~

To the messy lutefisk eater wearing a new suit:

To the wish that this fish
Will not spot your clothes
Raise it up near your nose—
Bite
Gulp
Down it goes!

~

A bit of history:

The gesture of clinking glasses began when early Christians wanted to produce a bell-like noise that would banish the devil, who was repelled by bells. Another explanation: Clinking glasses brings all five senses into play, so you taste, touch, see, smell, and—clink—hear the drink.

A joke for admirers of Ole and Lena:

Ole hated Tweet, Lena's pet parakeet. What a pest! Always picking at Ole's lutefisk. Whenever Ole would turn his head for a minute, the bird would swoop down and peck at Ole's plate. Maddening.

One time, though, one Syttende Mai, they were having lutefisk and Ole caught Tweet in the act. With a net he caught the bird and put it outside. He finished his lutefisk in peace, and then went out to mow the lawn.

About halfway through the job, when Ole was mowing around the bushes, he heard this terrible screech and saw feathers fly. He knew immediately what had happened. Tweet had nested in the bushes and had fallen into the path of the mower.

Ole picked up what was left of Tweet and went to tell Lena the bad news. "Uh, Lena," said Ole, sadly holding the messy remains.

"Goodness, Ole, what is that?" said Lena.

"Shredded Tweet."

To the lutefisk eater with a sensitive stomach:

Make way for this lutefisk
Forget being placid,
Spare my stomach and lower
A sip of antacid.

~

Some say lutefisk is the living end
But for me it's just a start
For once it's down, my innards turn
And burn what once was my heart.

~

To fishing friends long gone:

Oh, here's to this lutefisk,
This table and to wishing
That friends who have passed away
Could one more time go fishing.

~

A joke for all cowboys who love lutefisk:

A pair of Scandihoovian cowboys were crossing a windy mountain pass one winter day. One of cowboys, Lars, got down off his horse and pulled some slimey, cold cod out of his saddlebag. He was fixin' to make lutefisk back in camp. He then startled his buddy, Bjorn, when he kissed the fish.

"Whudd'ya do that fer?" asked a bewildered Bjorn.

"Got chapped lips," Lars replied.

Bjorn smacked his own lips and asked, "Does that help?"

Lars squinted into the wind and said, "Nope, but it keeps me from lickin' 'em."

A bit of history:

The Danes had much to do with the custom of drinking to one's health. When the Danes invaded Britain in the tenth century, British friends would toast each other's health and guard the drinker from harm while he tossed back the drink. What possible harm could come during a toast? No, not poisoning, but a good guess. This toast came about because of the Danish practice of slicing an enemy's throat while he drank.

To the wary guest, worried his neighbor will snitch his lutefisk:

Here's to my fork and here's to your hand—
may they never meet.

~

A toast to the aquavit-lutefisk alliance:

When lutefisk meets aquavit
It says, "How do you do?
Please numb their taste buds—do your job
And the guests will like me too."

~

A joke for those with a weakness for aquavit:

Nels likes his aquavit, perhaps a little too much. One November night after a wonderful lutefisk dinner, Nels was walking home. Well, he was actually staggering home because he had had too much aquavit. He fell on the ice and broke his leg.

Nels went to the doctor, who took one look at the broken leg and shook his head. "Nels, that broken leg will never be right," said the doc.

"Why not," said the worried Nels.

"Because it's your left leg."

A little joke for retired fishermen:

Bjorn and Magnus had been buddies at sea for years and years, catching cod, eating lutefisk, and drinking aquavit. But now they are retired. They still eat lutefisk and still drink aquavit. But they don't catch cod anymore and hardly ever see each other. Kinda sad. And when they do see each other, all they say is: "Long time, no sea."

~

To lutefisk dinners on a bad hair day:

For lutefisk and our hosts
I tame my hair with comb
Some strands go east, some go west
I wish they'd find one home.

~

Fine fish, good friends—these are the things
That loosen winter's grip
And lean us back in easy chairs
Our feet up as we sip.

~

To cod and to all who fish for cod:

May your vacations never coincide.

~

To eternity:

May we spend it in company as good as this.

~

Here's to cold nights, warm friends,
and lutefisk to serve them.

~

'Tis my *will* when I *die,* no tear shall be shed
No keening or wailing or holding of head
But place on my coffin a cut of lye cod
And write: He's prepared now to be with his God.

~

Lutefisk when you're hungry
Aquavit when you are dry
To lefse when you're homesick
And to heaven when you die.

~

A joke for outdoors people who like lutefisk:

Recently, Ole visited Alaska, where he read a notice posted by the State Department of Fish and Game advising hikers, hunters, and fishing folks to keep alert for bears while in the field. They advised extra precautions such as wearing little bells on clothing so as not to startle bears.

Ole kept reading and was a bit surprised when the department advised carrying a special lutefisk-scented spray created to drive bears—who have a very sensitive sense of smell—upwind and out of range of the odor.

Ole wondered where he could get some of this lutefisk spray, so he kept reading the notice. It said nothing more about the spray, but it advised people to be looking for fresh signs of bear scat. The scat of black bears, the advisory said, is smaller and contains a lot of berries and squirrel fur. Grizzle bear scat is bigger, has little bells in it, and smells like lutefisk.

~

Here's hoping you have a long life,
and lutefisk is the last scent you smell.

~

Here's to lutefisk:

It makes a lot of scents.

~

A bit of history:

Scandinavians, in the Vikings heyday (between 700 and 1,000 AD), would invite travelers into their home to warm up, rest, and be refreshed from a bowl of room-temperature beer, which was customarily on the table. This bowl was usually offered as a first gesture of welcome. This bowl was, and is still called, a skoal.

When you didn't have a bowl handy, you made do. The Scandinavians and the Scots had a practice of drinking mead or ale after battle by using the skull of a fallen enemy as the toasting vessel. In this case the bowl was first a brain bowl. Here's to hoping they washed it real well.

A bit of humor:

In a famous toast, George Bernard Shaw was called upon to deliver an after dinner toast on the subject of sex. At the turn of the century, this was considered a brazen topic, but Shaw was never one to shy away from a verbal challenge. He stood, raised a glass, and said: "It gives me great pleasure. . . ." and then he sat down.

～

To harried and horny lutefisk lovers:

Our joy slows our feast
And we dine with the least,
the smallest of woes in our head.
We bid "fast" adieu,
Bye-bye and yahoo!
Lutefisk—then off to our bed.

～

To our best friends:

You smell our worst lutefisk
And eat up our best.
You see all the bad in us
And still love the rest.

～

To my lover:

May your lutefisk be firm and hot
Your lefse soft and sweet
May you like them both, ya sure, why not?
You are just what you eat.

~

Days of ease and nights of pleasure
This lutefisk surpasses measure.

~

In the garden of life, may your spuds be not duds.

~

To my wife's lutefisk:

I miss it...
As often as I can.

~

Another visit with Ole and Lena:

Ole and Lena they've had their fights. Ya sure, especially in their courting days, they had some doozies. There was one when they were at the lutefisk dinner at Bethany Lutheran, and Ole said he liked to put melted butter on his lutefisk. Lena scoffed and said she liked to put a cream sauce on hers—and she couldn't understand anyone who didn't.

Well, one comment led to another, you know how lovers spat. And pretty soon Lena, wildly exasperated, yelled: "Ole, if you were my husband, I'd poison your lutefisk!"

Not to be outdone, Ole shouted: "And if I were your husband, I'd eat it!"

A tasteless joke for musicians:

Knute, the church organist, was new to lutefisk dinners. When the church had its annual lutefisk dinner, he gladly volunteered to entertain the folks who waited in the sanctuary for the dinner. When he arrived at the church to begin playing, he noticed the smell of lutefisk coming from the church basement. The cooks had been busy.

Knute went to the organ and was shocked to see a crystal glass bowl sitting on top of the organ. The bowl was filled with water. In the water floated, of all things, a condom!

"Oh, Knute, I'm glad you are here," said Miss Sivertson, the lutefisk cook. "I want to explain about that bowl."

"I would hope so, Miss Sivertson," huffed an indignant Knute.

"Oh, yes," she replied, "isn't it wonderful? I was walking downtown last fall and found this curious little package. It said to put it on your organ and keep it wet, and it would prevent disease. I did that at home on my organ, just like I did here with yours. And don't ya know, I think it is working. I haven't had a cold all winter!"

A joke for folks who like their aquavit too much:

Ole had a drinking problem years ago. In fact, he once saw a road sign that said "Drink Canada Dry." Next day, he moved to Vancouver.

~

May your lutefisk be flakier than your friends.

~

May you live long as long as you want,
and want lutefisk as long as you live.

~

A bit of history:

The custom of caroling from door-to-door derives from old wassails, which were toasts set to music.

To this sign at the crossroads to heaven:

To the Pearly Gates, go right.
To the lutefisk dinner, go left.
To Scandinavians: Make up your mind!

A joke for our hosts, who have it all:

During the cold and flu season, I asked my doctor: "What gift can I give to the hosts of a lutefisk dinner party I'm attending Saturday night?"

My doctor said, "What do your hosts need?"

"That's hard to say," I answered. "They're a couple who has everything."

"Oh, in that case," she said, "give them penicillin."

A bit of history:

The term *toast* was first used in the 17th century, when it was the custom to place a piece of toast or crouton in a drink. The idea was to improve the flavor of the drink. Water was often bad in those days, and alcohol was used as a preservative in foods and beverages. So people drank wine because they knew it was free of pathogens. Unfortunately, the wine often had a vinegary taste, so the toast served as a flavoring agent. At some weddings, a custom is that a glass of wine with toast in the bottom is passed for each lady to drink. The last to drink eats the toast and is considered lucky.

A bit of history:

The late 17th century was a time of odd toasting customs. Two examples: Students were known to grab a woman's shoe, using it to ladle wine from a common bowl and toasting the shoe's owner. Men also were known to show their affection for women by stabbing themselves in the arm, mixing their blood in the wine, and drinking to the lady. Be still my heart!

To lutefisk, lefse, and laughter:

Lutefisk in the fall
Lefse in the winter
Laughter through it all.

~

To sons of parents who are hard to please:

O, Maker of makers, please make me one
A lutefisk lover and a darn good son
To gain their approval, I'll eat this stuff
But, alas, knowing them, it won't be enough!

~

To point of view:

May your enemies be destitute of lutefisk.
May your enemies be knee-deep in lutefisk.

~

May the warmth of lutefisk dinners
survive the frosts of age.

~

May your lutefisk dinners be outnumbered
only by your coming pleasures.

~

To lutefisk:

It is God's way of compensating us for growing old.

~

To our children:

Eat your lutefisk. If you don't, you'll grow up
to be twice as wide and half as wise as us.

~

A toast for the rare occasion when the lutefisk is bad at church dinners:

To the faithful gathered at these tables,
congratulations on having had such a religious
experience. This lutefisk is a living hell!

~

To the worried lutefisk cook:

Do not fret, my dear
Don't cry in your beer
For worry rusts the blade.
Make meatballs as well
It will turn out swell,
Kick back, you've got it made.

~

To lutefisk feasts, which will add to your mirth,
Pile it on, eat up, this will add to your girth.

∿

Slow to make enemies
Quick to make friends
Lutefisk lovers are
Tops till the end.

∿

A bit of history:

"Here's mud in your eye!" is a somewhat silly, meaning-less toast today, but it has an interesting history. An older version ends with ". . . while I look over your lovely sweetheart!"

A later version developed with the opening of the American West. A pioneering farmer leaving the East would stop at a local tavern to say good-bye to friends, who would toast "Here's mud in your eye!" They were hoping that the farmer would find soft, rich soil to farm—soil that the plough would spit up as specks of mud in the farmer's eye.

Live as long as you wish
Wish as long as you live
For lutefisk, lefse, and love.

～

To lutefisk and self-esteem:

My lutefisk is flakey
My flatbread is so dry
As you can see, I eat them
'Cuz so am I.

～

To expectant parents:

The grocier said, "One lutefisk
For every baby born!"
So when the due date came along
The child came in the morn.
The grocier said, "Oh, what a peach,
There is none to compare."
"We're mighty glad," the parents said,
"The peach is not a pair!"

～

A joke for golfers:

At the Lutefisk Open in Rochester, Minn., Bjorn, who is known for his modesty, walked out on to the first tee wearing two pairs of pants.

The rest of his foursome looked at each other in wonder, but thought, "To each his own." However, by the fourth hole, a 158-yard par 3, the curiosity got the best of everyone. After all, it was a 90-degree day!

Finally, right before Bjorn was set to tee off on this par 3, Carl asked, "Say, Bjorn, vhy you vearing two pairs of pants, then?"

Bjorn waggled his club, eyed the flagstick, and answered, "In case I get a hole in one."

To coffee lovers:

Fresh coffee comes with lutefisk
But Ole's feeling down.
"It tastes like dirt!" he shouts to all
And Lena turns to frown
She says, "It should, ya dunderhead
That coffee is fresh ground."

~

How does a deaf cod hear? With a herring aid.

~

To trying too hard to help:

When friends came for their lutefisk
But left the church in doubt
The problem was they talked to Sven
And said, "Please help me out."
He tried to help, oh ya, he did
But shucks, he couldn't win
He said, "Ya sure, no problem, then
Which way did you come in?"

~

A joke about flattery:

Ruth went to the lutefisk dinner all alone because her best friend came down with the flu. Ruth sat in the church pew, waiting for her number to be called so she could be seated for lutefisk.

She noticed a jar of peanuts at the end of each pew. She looked around and then took a handful to munch on. It wasn't long before she heard a little voice whisper, "You have such pretty eyes."

Ruth looked but nobody was sitting anywhere near her. A moment later, the little voice whispered, "You are such a nice person."

Again she looked around trying to find who had said this to her. Again, nobody was close by.

"That dress flatters you," said the little voice. Ruth looked, saw no one near, but was relieved when Pastor Larson came down the center aisle.

"Oh, Pastor Larson, thank goodness," said Ruth. "I have been hearing this little voice saying the sweetest things, but I cannot figure out who's saying them."

"Not to worry, Ruth, you are not going crazy," said Pastor Larson. "It's the peanuts. They're comlimentary."

A timely joke:

What are the odds of your church starting its lutefisk dinner at 12:50? About 10 to 1.

A joke for sensitive male lutefisk eaters:

The Vikings were known more for whacking heads than for waxing philosophical. But they did have a sensitive side, especially when they ate lutefisk. In fact, one group of Vikings, high on loads of lutefisk, stayed up all night hugging and supporting each other as they contemplated the sun, its energy, its light.

"Such wonder," they said, "but why does it abandon us each night? And why does it return?"

It was one of those shared experiences that was, like, so totally special. Not only did these Vikings find another side of themselves, but in the morning the answers to their questions dawned on them.

To the Vikings:

To lutefisk and Vikings passed
Who pigged out when it snowed.
How can we talk, reach you at last?
But one way—Norse code.

~

To my friend, who is like a good potato:
You're always there when the chips are down.

~

If overeating lutefisk
Is your flaw tonight
Go out the door, I do insist
Please go, and please don't fight.
And set your keister by the street
To "curb" your appetite!

~

To those worried about their waistline:

Here's hoping you don't eat too much lutefisk.
It could make you thick to your stomach.

~

50

A little joke that will bowl you over:

Since this is a lutefisk dinner party, I suppose you're
not interested in a joke about bowling.

No, spare us.

~

To lutefisk, Adam, and Eve:

Lutefisk to lift your humor
Humor to Adam whose day was long
Long because there was no Eve.

~

To kissing and lutefisk:

Lutefisk made couples kiss
But what happened in the fog?
They tried to kiss but they mist,
So they sighed and walked the dog.

~

A joke about lumberjacks and lutefisk:

They have banned lutefisk from the north woods. It seems lumberjacks loved lutefisk, to the point of distraction. They couldn't keep their mind on their work. Too often, when they cooked lutefisk as the trees were being felled, the yell of the lumberjacks was "Tim. . . ."

~

To tuba players and their offspring:

If your lutefisk could play a horn
It would be a tuba
When two tubas have a baby born
The baby's called a nuba.
The first words out of little nuba?
No, no, it's not "Ma-ma."
The first words out of little nuba—
That's right, it's "Ooom-Papa!"

~

Here's to Melville's lutefisk masterpiece: *Moby Ick.*

~

One last Ole and Lena joke:

Lena has always liked it that Ole has been a giving person, ever since he was a kid. Lena, she remembers when they were dating in school, and one night when they were necking out on the point, they were wondering about their fates in life. Ole wondered if he was meant to catch cod and make lutefisk when he grew up.

"You a fisherman, Ole?" said Lena, incredulous. "Nope. That's not you. You're too generous, and that job would make you *sell fish.*"

"Hmmm. I never thought about it that way," said Ole. "And what about you, Lena dear, what do you want to be?"

"Oh, I don't know, Ole, maybe a doctor or nurse," she said.

"Gee, Lena," said Ole, scratching his head, "I don't think you have the *patients* for it."

~

To lutefisk:

You're the sail in my love boat
You are the captain and crew
But cooked too long in the pot—
Then you are mutiny stew!

To bright endings:

The undertaker thought Knute died
From too much lutefisk.
A closer look, though, and he spied
That varnish killed him—ISH!
How odd, how odd, and what a sight!
And Knute wrote his last wish:
"A varnished gut may not be right
But what a bright finish."

~

To two eyes and one nose:

The eyes, with their unassailable wisdom and
vision, had it right when they said to each other at
the lutefisk dinner: "Just between you and me,
there is something that smells."

~

A joke for the moonstruck:

Ole had eaten too much lutefisk and decided to walk it off. It was a beautiful, clear winter night. The moon was full and silvery, and Ole looked at it peacefully. He had always wanted to go to the moon when he was a kid.

Hey, he thought, why can't I do it now? Lots of people are going up these days, even old guys like John Glenn.

So he called NASA down at Cape Kennedy and said he wanted to go to the moon.

"Sorry, sir," was the answer, "but the moon is full just now."

A tired joke:

Whenever Thor ate lutefisk, he got heartburn and didn't sleep too well. But he loved the stuff, so one night after eating a big helping of lutefisk at the First Lutheran Church dinner, he stretched his long body out at the edge of the bed.

Ingrid looked at him funny and said, "Thor, why are you sleeping at the edge of the bed?"

He said, "So I can drop off to sleep."

~

To lutefisk:

See what happens when you lye to cod?

~

To Lazarus and lutefisk:

Both came back from the dead.

~

To life:

If I had to do it over again, I'd eat lutefisk sooner.

A dairy joke:

After the lutefisk dinner at Trinity Lutheran, all the farmers gather and swap lies. Something to do, ya know. Well, Knute, who is a pretty good dairy farmer, he starts talking about the secret to getting a lot of milk from his bossies is to give them coffee.

"Coffee!" says Sven. "Why, I never heard of such a thing."

"Ya, it's true," says Knute. "Except you don't give 'em coffee right after they have their calves," warns Knute.

"What do you give them then?" asks Sven.

"Decaf, of course."

~

To the tired guest:

'Tis hard to tell which is best
Friends, Food, Drink, or Rest.

~

To endings, which are inevitable:

Here's to lutefisk! Now that I have learned to make the most of it, most of it is gone.

~

To lutefisk:

It doesn't build character—it reveals it.

YOUR TOASTS!

Do you have a favorite toast that you use at lutefisk dinners? How about a favorite lutefisk or lefse joke? We'd love to see them!

We are collecting these toasts and jokes so that they can be published.

If you want to contribute your wit—and be given credit in the book—please write your toast or joke below. Thanks!

_____

_____

_____

_____

_____

_____

_____

_____

Please mail to:
Conrad Henry Press
5205 Knox Ave. S.
Minneapolis, MN 55419-1041

Fax:
612-926-0463

E-mail:
glegwold@lutefisk.com

ORDER FORM

Please send me _____ *copies of* The Last Toast to Lutefisk.
Please send me _____ *copies of* The Last Word on Lutefisk.
Please send me _____ *copies of* The Last Word on Lefse.

Fax orders: 612-926-0463
Telephone orders: Call toll free 1(888) LUTEFIS = 1(888) 588-3347.
Please have your credit card ready.
Postal orders: Conrad Henry Press
          5205 Knox Ave. S.
          Minneapolis, MN 55419-1041
Web site: http://www.lutefisk.com
E-mail: glegwold@lutefisk.com

I understand that if I am not satisfied with these books, I may return them for a full refund—no questions asked.

Cost: $8.95 + tax + shipping for The Last Toast to Lutefisk
     $14.95 + tax + shipping for The Last Word on Lutefisk.
     $9.95 + tax + shipping for The Last Word on Lefse.
Tax: Please add 7% to the cost of the book if the book is shipped to
     Minneapolis; St. Paul; Rochester, Minn.; Mankato, Minn.; and
     Hermantown, Minn.
     Add 7.5% to the cost of the book if the book is shipped to Cook
     County, Minn.
     Add 6.5% to the cost of the book if the book is shipped to Minnesota
     locations other than those mentioned above
Shipping: $3.50 for the first book. For each additional book, add $.50 (U.S. only).

Please send the book(s) to:

Name: _____

Address: _____

City: _____ *State:* _____ *Zip:* _____

Payment: ☐ *Check*   ☐ *Credit card*

Type of card: _____ *Name on card:* _____

Card number: _____ *Exp. date:* _____